Developing a Business Case

Pocket Mentor Series

The Pocket Mentor Series offers immediate solutions to common challenges managers face on the job every day. Each book in the series is packed with handy tools, self-tests, and real-life examples to help you identify your strengths and weaknesses and hone critical skills. Whether you're at your desk, in a meeting, or on the road, these portable guides enable you to tackle the daily demands of your work with greater speed, savvy, and effectiveness.

Books in the series:

Becoming a New Manager

Coaching People

Creating a Business Plan

Delegating Work

Developing Employees

Dismissing an Employee

Executing Innovation

Executing Strategy

Focusing on Your Customer

Fostering Creativity

Giving Feedback

Giving Presentations

Hiring an Employee

Improving Business Processes

Laying Off Employees

Leading People

Leading Teams

Making Decisions

Managing Change

Managing Crises

Managing Difficult Interactions

Managing Diversity

Managing Projects

Managing Stress

Managing Time

Managing Teams

Managing Up

Measuring Performance

Negotiating Outcomes

Performance Appraisal

Persuading People

Preparing a Budget

Preparing a Business Plan

Retaining Employees

Running Meetings

Setting Goals

Shaping Your Career

Thinking Strategically

Understanding Finance

Understanding Marketing

Writing for Business

Developing a Business Case

Expert Solutions to Everyday Challenges

Harvard Business Review Press

Boston, Massachusetts

Library of Congress Cataloging-in-Publication Data

    Developing a business case : expert solutions to everyday challenges.
       p. cm. — (Pocket mentor series)
    Includes bibliographical references.
    ISBN 978-1-4221-2976-0 (pbk. : alk. paper)
    1. Decision making.   2. Business presentations.   I. Harvard Business
School. Press.
    HD30.23.D475 2010
    658.4'03—dc22

                         2010020769

The paper used in this publication meets the requirements of the American National
Standard for Permanence of Paper for Publications and Documents in Libraries and
Archives Z39.48-1992.

Contents

Step 6: Craft a Plan for Implementing Your Idea 57

Tips for ensuring that your proposed alternative can be put into action.

Step 7: Communicate Your Case 65

Techniques for presenting your case to decision makers.

Tips and Tools

Tools for Developing a Business Case   73

Worksheets for identifying alternatives, tracking implementation of your idea, ensuring that you've taken all the right steps for creating a business case, and documenting an actual business case.

Mentor's Message: The Advantages of a Solid Business Case

As a manager, you may often spot opportunities to help your team, department, and even your entire organization meet important business goals. When you identify such an opportunity, you may quickly think of a course of action that you believe would enable you to seize the opportunity. And you may feel compelled to implement that course of action.

That's understandable—but it's also dangerous. It means you haven't considered a wide enough range of alternatives for capturing the opportunity you've identified. This is where developing a business case comes in. A business case is a tool for identifying and comparing multiple alternatives for pursuing an opportunity and then proposing the one course of action that will create the most value.

A well-developed business case can help you present a convincing argument for a particular solution to key stakeholders whose support you would need to implement your proposed solution. Preparing a business case also forces you to take a disciplined approach to generating ideas for how best to capture the opportunity and comparing the strengths and weaknesses of the alternatives. When you take the time and care to build a solid business case, you arrive at a better decision with greater impact. You also stand a far greater chance of winning the support you need to put your choice into action.

This book walks you through the steps needed to build a strong business case. In it, you'll find a wealth of ideas, tools, and examples for defining the opportunity you want to pursue, identifying alternatives for seizing the opportunity, gathering data on your alternatives and estimating the time frames for each of them, analyzing the data you've collected so you can compare your alternatives' pros and cons, selecting the best choice and assessing any risks associated with it, crafting a plan for implementing your chosen course of action, and communicating your case effectively to stakeholders.

All this may sound like a lot to learn—but it's actually quite manageable. And it's well worth the time. So let's get started!

June Paradise Maul, Mentor

President of Advantage Value, a consulting and education company, Dr. June Paradise Maul has experience leading large-scale change as well as line organizations, having been Chief Learning Officer at Qwest and having held senior management positions at AT & T. Dr. Maul has taught executive development programs in corporations. She has also taught graduate-level business and leadership programs—including strategic planning, balanced scorecard, strategic leadership, virtual workplace, decision making, and creative resourcing. She is invited to speak and consult globally on leadership, strategic planning, decision making, and creative resourcing. Dr. Maul is also president of LifestyleK9's, a small international business that breeds and trains German Shepherds as working dogs (www.lifestylek9.com). Dr. Maul received her Bachelor of Science in Asian Studies and Geology from M.I.T. and her doctorate in Science and Humanities from Rutgers.

Developing a Business Case: The Basics

What Is a
Business Case?

erhaps you've been managing a project and you've concluded that acquiring some new software would help your company cut costs and increase efficiencies. Or maybe you want to hire several new employees or buy a new piece of equipment for your group.

You've presented your proposal to your boss, and he responded, "You'll need to make the business case for it before we can consider it."

You're happy to oblige—but you're not sure what, precisely, a business case consists of or how to go about creating one. You wonder, "Does he mean a business *plan*?" But a business case differs in important ways from a business plan. Your first step in building a case for your great idea is to understand the difference.

Business case versus business plan

A *business case* answers the question "What happens if we take this course of action?" For example, if your unit is considering expanding sales to a new market, your boss might ask, "Which of three alternative markets should we invest in to create the most value? And should we even make this investment?"

A *business plan,* on the other hand, describes how an organization or business unit intends to navigate successfully through its own unique competitive environment. Business plans feature long-range projections of revenues, expenses, business strategy, and other information. Typically, managers and executives use business plans to secure financing from investors or to plan strategy execution for an organization or business.

When you should create a business case

In many ways, the process of building a business case is similar to solving a problem. For example, suppose you don't have enough staff to accomplish your responsibilities, or you believe that your company's competitors use more efficient processes that allow them to have lower costs than your firm does. Developing a business case would not only help you identify potential solutions to such problems, but also help you sell your ideas to key decision makers.

A business case is useful when you want to

- Demonstrate the value a proposed product or service would generate for your organization

- Prioritize projects within your group and identify which ones to eliminate

- Demonstrate the value of a product or service to a customer to make a sale

- Obtain additional resources for a new project, initiative, or organization

- Modify an existing offering

- Invest in a new capability, such as a software program or training

- Decide whether to outsource a particular function

A complex document

As you might imagine, building a business case for a relatively simple decision—such as whether to buy a new copier for your department and, if so, which one to select—is a pretty straightforward process. When you're making a case for a more expensive, complex course of action, however, the process requires more thought.

As you'll discover, this book presents a fairly sophisticated example for illustrative purposes—so you can see how the entire process of creating a business case unfolds. In your role, you may not need to gather as much information as the protagonist in the example must gather, and you may not need to use complex numerical analysis. Whereas a business case similar to the example used in the topic may take ten to fifteen days to complete, a simpler business case may take only a few hours.

> *It's not the plan that is important, it's the planning.*
> —Dr. Graeme Edwards

Seven steps to a business case

Still, it is important to distinguish between the process of building a business case and the *product* you deliver to decision makers and stakeholders. The product is a document or presentation. Many organizations have their own templates and specific guidelines for how to create this product—including how to format the information, how to treat graphics, and so forth.

This book focuses on the *process* of defining the opportunity, identifying the alternatives, gathering the necessary information, analyzing the alternatives, and preparing to sell your ideas. After all, building a business case is about identifying and considering multiple alternatives before making a well-informed recommendation to support one option that will create value for the organization and often its stakeholders. The creation of a document or presentation is the final step in this process—and it can happen only after you've completed the earlier steps.

Regardless of the format of your business case, you can use the following steps to prepare it:

- **Step 1: Define the opportunity.** Describe the situation and the business objectives that your proposal will affect.

- **Step 2: Identify the alternatives.** Brainstorm multiple approaches and then choose three to four to analyze.

- **Step 3: Gather data and estimate time frame.** Obtain information about each alternative and estimate how long each option will take to implement.

- **Step 4: Analyze the alternatives.** Analyze how your options will affect the business objectives you've defined.

- **Step 5: Make a choice and assess the risk.** Make a recommendation based on your analyses, and consider how you will mitigate any risks associated with your recommendation.

- **Step 6: Create a plan for implementing your idea.** Identify, at a high level, how you will achieve your goals and who will be accountable for each milestone. Spell out when you expect to see benefits.

- **Step 7: Communicate your case.** Create a document or a presentation, or both, to sell your recommendation to decision makers.

You will need to complete each of these steps to build a strong business case. However, the depth of analysis and extent of documentation necessary to support your case will likely vary depending on the proposed initiative's scope, costs, organizational impact, and risk.

Step 1: Define the Opportunity

To define the opportunity you want to pursue, you need to

- Identify a problem or opportunity
- Craft an opportunity statement
- Identify your business objectives in pursuing the opportunity
- Prioritize your objectives
- Assign metrics to your objectives

In the pages that follow, we'll look at each of these tasks more closely.

Identifying a problem or opportunity

The first step in building a business case is identifying the problem you want to solve or the opportunity you want to seize. Even if your boss has the idea and asks you to build the business case for it, you will still need a solid understanding of the issue at hand.

Consider how you would describe the following situation, which will be used as an example throughout this book:

Satellite Electronics' new strategy will require that 200 sales staff learn how to identify customers' needs and define the best solution, or set of products and services, to meet those needs. A competitor that recently adopted this approach has seen its sales per headcount increase from 10 percent to 12 percent.

What Would YOU Do?

Running with the Big Dogs

ANATOLE HEADS THE PRODUCT development group at BigDogDuds, a company that makes fashionably designed accessories for dogs, including collars, leashes, beds, and food bowls. BigDogDuds' leadership team recently decided to expand the company's product line to include accessories for "dogs who are on the go." Product ideas include ear protection for dogs whose owners are general-aviation pilots and want to take their dogs flying, goggles for dogs who ride in open vehicles like pickup trucks and Jeeps, and mildew- and odor-resistant collars for dogs who swim a lot.

To support this new strategy, Anatole's group will need to step up its product development and design efforts. One day, Anatole goes in to see his boss, Charlie, to get his thoughts on how best to expand the group's work. He happens to catch Charlie on a busy day. Charlie's distracted, pawing through a pile of papers on his desk, and barks at Anatole: "Just do a business case for hiring a couple of people to help you." Anatole nods and heads back to his office . . . but he's not sure this is the best course of action.

What would YOU do? The mentor will suggest a solution in *What You COULD Do.*

Sydney Starr heads the training and development group at Satellite. Her group is already stretched to its limit with current assignments. Her boss has told her that no current projects can be eliminated or delayed. Sydney is grappling with the problem of how to best support the sales organization during its transition to the new strategy.

Developing an opportunity statement

Once you identify the problem or opportunity at hand, develop a statement that describes the benefits that will come with solving the problem or seizing the opportunity. In other words, answer the question "How will my group, unit, or company benefit from spending resources to address this issue?"

A strong opportunity statement for Sydney would be as follows:

The training and development group will help increase revenue at Satellite by enabling the sales group to move from a product-selling to a solutions-selling approach.

When drafting your own statement, be sure to address the situation as an opportunity rather than a problem. Also, avoid the common mistake of defining the opportunity by describing your preferred solution. For example, Sydney might be tempted to describe the issue as "I need two more headcount to support the new sales strategy." This statement is too limited and would prevent Sydney from considering alternative solutions.

When you confront a problem, you begin to solve it.
—Rudy Giuliani

What You COULD Do.

Remember Anatole's concern about his boss's proposed plan of action?

Here's what the mentor suggests:

Anatole's boss, Charlie, made the common mistake of seeing a business case as a means to justify a desired course of action (in this instance, the hiring of several employees to help Anatole's group step up its product development actions). When managers take this approach, they miss out on the opportunity to consider a broad range of possible ways to achieve important business goals.

Anatole shouldn't follow Charlie's lead blindly. Instead, he should build a case around how his group can best support BigDogDuds' new strategy. By thinking about the larger opportunity, instead of looking at just one way of approaching it, Anatole stands a chance of coming up with an even better recommendation than what Charlie proposed. At the very least, a broader analysis of possible courses of action would confirm that Charlie's proposed solution is, in fact, the best course of action.

As part of the process, Anatole should consider multiple alternatives, including remaining with the status quo. For example, his analysis might reveal that BigDogDuds would do better by eliminating some current development projects than trying to expand the staff to take on new ones.

Identifying your business objectives

Once you've written your opportunity statement, identify the most relevant business objectives you hope to achieve by pursuing this opportunity. Beyond the obvious financial gains, such as cost savings or increased sales, consider how seizing the opportunity you've defined will enable your company to reach important goals. To find out what your company considers important, examine the key business metrics it tracks and reports—such as employee morale, customer loyalty, environmental responsibility, revenues, costs, and so forth. Often, a company's performance measurement system—for instance, a balanced scorecard or a dashboard—documents your organization's high-level metrics.

Even if some of your company's key objectives are difficult to measure in dollar terms—such as improved employee satisfaction—don't shy away from considering them. Be sure to list all the key objectives that might be relevant for your project.

Prioritizing your objectives

Now prioritize these objectives, choosing three or four to analyze. How can you narrow your list? Ask yourself whose support you would need to implement your ideas, and who would be affected if your ideas were put into action. Consider how these stakeholders tend to make decisions and what business results are important to them. Consider which ones are priorities for your organization's senior leaders.

For example, in the Satellite scenario:

- The vice president of finance might be most concerned with cost reduction, revenue increase, or profitability improvement.

- The vice president of sales might be particularly concerned with customer satisfaction and revenue growth.

- The vice president of human resources (HR) might care most about employee satisfaction, which drives turnover of sales staff.

After assessing these preferences, Sydney might identify the following objectives:

- Increase profitability and revenues.

- Improve customer satisfaction.

- Reduce employee turnover.

Assigning metrics to your objectives

The next step is to identify metrics for each of the objectives you've defined. Later, once you've determined your alternatives, you'll use these metrics to measure the impact of each course of action on your chosen objectives.

In the Satellite example, Sydney ties each of her business objectives to metrics as follows:

- **Increase profitability and revenues.** Sydney decides it will be important to measure the impact of alternative proposals on the metric "sales revenue per person." Because both costs and revenues affect profitability, Sydney also decides to measure the one-time and ongoing costs associated with each alternative.

- **Improve customer satisfaction.** Satellite uses a performance management system that includes customer satisfaction as a metric, so Sydney decides she will use the existing metric. She also decides to ask the sales and marketing departments if they use metrics such as "customer retention"—on the assumption that the more satisfied customers are, the more likely they are to keep doing business with the company. Because loyal customers often buy more, Sydney also considers using the metric "repeat sales."

- **Reduce employee turnover.** Because employee satisfaction affects turnover, Sydney decides to ask her colleagues in human resources to provide her with data from the annual employee satisfaction survey as well as information about employee turnover. She'll use the ratings from the survey as her "employee satisfaction" metric in addition to the existing "turnover" metric. She also opts to use "cost of employee turnover" as a metric. The cost of employee turnover derives from hiring and training costs as well as any loss in productivity while new hires get up to speed. For a new sales employee, lost productivity takes the form of lost sales dollars.

For any business objective, there are many potential metrics from which to choose. In addition to the financial and nonfinancial metrics described above, there are metrics based on time, quality, work habits, employee development, and so forth that may be appropriate for your business case. Also, your company may already be tracking metrics that are useful for your business case. If appropriate metrics currently exist, there's no need to invent new ones.

Step 2: Identify the Alternatives

Now that you've defined the opportunity you want to pursue, you need to identify alternative courses of action you could take to seize that opportunity. This step comprises the following tasks:

- Generate a list of options or alternative courses of action.

- Gather input from stakeholders.

- Narrow your choices down to a few especially promising ones.

Let's examine each of these tasks in more detail.

Generating a list of options

While building a business case, it's vital to brainstorm a full set of alternatives rather than latching on to the first one or two good ideas that occur to you. The following pitfalls can prevent you from developing a comprehensive list of alternatives:

- Restricting the list of choices to the first solutions you consider

- Having a limiting mind-set, such as believing that "consultants should never be used" or that "consultants should always be used"

- Having a strong preference for a particular solution at the outset of the process and therefore failing to explore additional possibilities

- Failing to consider the status quo (the current condition) as an alternative

To avoid these traps, convene a group of stakeholders and ask them to brainstorm ideas with you. These stakeholders are the people who would be affected by the outcome of your proposal—but they could be inside or outside your organization. Record the results of the brainstorming on a flip chart or white board, *without* judging them or discussing their potential pros and cons. Your goal is to generate as many feasible alternatives as possible.

Gathering input

Since a big part of building a business case is selling your idea, it makes sense to identify and talk with stakeholders early in the process so they feel more involved. They may also provide ideas and information you would not have thought of. You'll also learn what they value most—thus, you can better appeal to their interests in your final presentation.

When Sydney conducts her brainstorming session, she invites her team members as well as key people in sales, finance, and HR. The participants come up with a long list of ideas for enabling the training group to help sales adopt the new solutions-selling strategy. These ideas include "add FTEs [full-time employees] in training department," "hire curriculum consultants," "use outside classroom facilitators," "cancel low-priority existing projects," and many other possibilities.

After generating a list of alternatives, meet with other stakeholders to get additional ideas for alternatives, as well as insights into the possibilities you've generated so far. Talking with trusted advisers at this stage is also prudent.

For example, suppose that after talking with other stakeholders Sydney discovers that Satellite's finance and human resources departments have implemented a hiring freeze during the current fiscal year. In this case, she could decide to omit the alternative "add FTEs in training department" and focus instead on ideas such as using a training consulting firm or hiring outside classroom facilitators. Even if she decides to keep the FTE alternative under consideration, she'll want to show why she believes it's an important possibility and how it compares to using a consultancy or hiring outside contractors.

In the end, Sydney ends up with the following list of alternatives:

1. Try to support the new sales strategy with the existing training staff (the status quo option).

2. Add two permanent employees in the training group who will focus on implementing the new training.

3. Add two contractors to focus on the implementation.

4. Hire a consulting firm to do the work.

5. Borrow people from sales to help implement the training.

Always think outside the box and embrace opportunities
that appear, wherever they might be.
—Lakshmi Mittal

"Steps for building support for your business case" provides additional ideas for using communication with stakeholders to establish support for your case.

Steps for building support for your business case

1. **Identify key stakeholders and decision makers.** Consider who will be affected by your idea. Also, who controls the resources you will need to implement it? Ask yourself how these people might respond to your idea.

2. **Ask for input from stakeholders early in the process.** Arrange an informal meeting with key stakeholders to ask for their advice on the ideas you have explored in your business case. Your goal in these meetings is not to present the case but just to discuss it. Before you meet with stakeholders, anticipate their concerns and be prepared to answer their questions. During your meetings, try to uncover the opportunities and issues that are most important. What do they care about? How will they benefit from your idea? Have them identify any gaps they see; it's better to get input on your plan's shortcomings now than have them pointed out later in the process.

3. **Incorporate any feedback into your case.** The discussions you have with stakeholders will help bring to the surface information that you can use to improve your proposal and help secure approval. For example, you may learn which business objectives are most important to key decision makers. You might then evaluate your options against these objectives. In addition, you may learn other information that is critical for your case.

4. **Ask for input from trusted advisers.** As you build your case, show your preliminary work to trusted advisers and mentors in your informal network. Ask the individuals to look for holes in your analysis and to suggest questions that decision makers might raise. Revise your case based on the input you receive.

5. **Collect benchmarks on other organizations.** As you build the case, do some benchmarking research, identifying other organizations that may have focused on this same opportunity. Find other organizations that have implemented a solution. You may be able to find out the solutions they considered and understand why they selected their particular approach. This process often yields valuable data you can use to sell your business case.

6. **Create multiple delivery formats for your case.** When you're ready to sell your recommendation, you'll want to create different versions of your business case for different stakeholders. For example, you might want to have a detailed document including all of your assumptions and calculations for your advisers and your own use. Prepare a higher-level slide presentation for communicating your idea to decision makers. You might also want to create an executive summary tailored

to address specific stakeholder concerns and interests for groups that would be affected by your recommendation. You may also want to develop a "one-minute elevator pitch"—a short statement describing the opportunity, the solution, and the expected value and impact. Your elevator pitch can be useful when you're talking to executives and meeting with stakeholders.

Narrowing your choices

Once you have received input from stakeholders, it's time to narrow your list of alternatives down to the two or three options—in addition to the status quo—that will best address your business objectives and stakeholders' needs. Strategies for narrowing your choices include the following:

- Combine any alternatives that could reasonably be implemented together.

- Eliminate elaborate, high-risk options.

- Favor the easy-to-implement solution over the complex and difficult.

Don't spend too much time agonizing over this step. Instead, go with your intuition about which choices seem the most feasible and likely to meet your objectives. At this stage, you will likely want to depend more on your hunches and professional judgment than a careful analysis of each alternative.

Consider Sydney's case: Since she knows that Satellite executives will resist adding permanent headcount immediately, she decides to combine her original options 2 and 3 into a single solution: hiring two contractors with the intent that they may become permanent employees in a year. She also knows that sales is already under-staffed, so she deletes option 5 (borrowing people from sales to implement the training).

Thus, her final list of alternatives is as follows:

1. Hire a consulting firm to develop and deliver the training.

2. Add two contractors to provide the training, with the option to hire them as permanent employees after a year, if necessary.

3. Try to implement the new training with the existing staff (the status quo option).

Step 3: Gather Data and Estimate Time Frame

O nce you've identified alternatives for pursuing your opportunity, it's time to gather data on your alternatives and estimate time frames for implementing them. It's good to start by identifying the information you'll need to gather.

Identifying the information you need

List all the information you'll need to compare your choices. How do you determine the needed information? Look again at the metrics you've chosen for each of your business objectives. Ask yourself what data you'll need to gather for each metric.

For example, Sydney would start by examining the business metrics she defined. Keep in mind that Sydney's business case is relatively complex. Depending on the scope of your own business case, you may not need to gather nearly as much supporting data as Sydney.

Sydney might want to obtain the following data for the metrics she plans to track:

- **Sales revenue per person:** the number of dollars in sales each person would generate for each scenario

- **Cost of each alternative:** the one-time and ongoing costs associated with each of her three choices

- **Customer satisfaction:** historical customer-satisfaction ratings from the company's performance management system, plus anticipated ratings for each scenario

- **Customer retention:** historical customer-retention rates from the sales and marketing departments, plus anticipated retention rates for each scenario

- **Repeat sales:** figures on the repeat sales typically generated by retained customers, and estimates of how many customers would be retained given each of the three scenarios

- **Employee satisfaction:** historical employee-satisfaction data from HR surveys, plus educated guesses about how employee satisfaction might change in each scenario

- **Turnover:** historical turnover rates, and estimates of how each scenario might affect turnover

- **Cost of employee turnover:** typical costs of hiring and training sales people, plus information from sales about how much revenue is lost when a new sales employee is ramping up

Wherever possible, you should start by obtaining historical or typical data. You'll then want to forecast changes in those data that would result from each of the alternatives you're comparing.

Collecting the data

The information you want probably won't all be in one place. You'll have to do some digging. Sources to consult include the following:

- Internal colleagues in HR, finance, or other departments that might have access to key business performance metrics

- Colleagues and friends outside your organization who have proposed a similar initiative or project

- Industry journals and reports

- Industry experts

- The Internet

- Consulting firms with expertise in the choices you are considering

Consider consulting several sources for each piece of information, to get the best estimates possible.

> *The best preparation for good work tomorrow*
> *is to do good work today.*
> —Elbert Hubbard

See "Tips for gathering data" for additional ideas.

Tips for gathering data

- Define the categories of information you'll need to compare your options. Use the business objectives you selected to help guide your process.
- Make a list of the specific questions you want answered, such as "How much will it cost to replace a sales employee?" or "How will customer satisfaction be affected by this alternative?"

- Be prepared to add to your list of questions. As you gather information, you'll probably identify additional factors that could affect your alternatives. For example, meeting with a colleague in operations may inspire you to consider elements you would never have thought of on your own.
- Document your assumptions and sources as you go. It's easy to forget where you found a particular piece of information. Keeping a list will help you explain your logic if someone asks.
- Make sure your estimates are realistic. Consider whether the data you find sound correct. If not, seek additional estimates.
- For each piece of information, consult multiple sources, such as several colleagues in different departments, to get the best estimates possible.
- Once you have gathered the data, ask for input from individuals in departments that would be affected by your recommendation to make sure you haven't overlooked anything.

Setting a time frame

Once you've gathered your data, estimate a time frame for implementing the initiative and achieving the benefits of the opportunity you've defined, given each of the alternatives you're considering. Also consider how long it will be until the project delivers its estimated benefits—it may be a year or two, or longer.

In Sydney's case, she would gauge how long it would take her group to provide the solutions-selling training in each of the three scenarios she's exploring, as well as the time needed for the sales force to realize 100 percent of its target benefits.

To set a time frame, ask:

- When would the initiative get under way?

- Would it be phased in over the course of one year, three years, or more?

- Would it be synchronized with calendar years, fiscal years, or other initiatives?

- Would it have a clear end point at which all its benefits would be generated?

Setting a time frame requires a lot of estimating. For example, in the Satellite scenario, Sydney calculates, in rough terms, how long it would take to provide the sales training with her current staff versus how long it would take if she hired a consulting firm or used two contractors with the option of hiring them permanently. Next, she estimates how long it will take the sales force to get up to speed and realize target benefits. Finally, she projects out a year or two for the time until the benefits of the project will be fully realized and provide competitive advantage.

Documenting your estimates and assumptions

When you make estimates like these, record the information you're using and the assumptions you're making. Documenting in this way will enable you to explain your reasoning to anyone who asks.

For example, Sydney assumes that Satellite's customers would respond to the solutions-selling approach in the same way that its competitors' customers did. She can get these revenue-increase assumptions from the internal group (e.g., finance, strategy) who put together the rationale for moving to this strategy.

Among other estimates, Sydney will also need to approximate the financial costs for each alternative. For example:

- **The consulting option:** She would start by asking the consulting firm for fees and costs it has incurred in the past, and then look to similar projects she might have carried out in the past.

- **The contractor option:** She would ask the hiring manager about the costs associated with hiring contractors, and then consider what turning them into employees might cost.

- **The status quo option:** She would build in the cost for her current staff to do the work.

Once Sydney has the numbers she needs, she'll document her sources. She'll want to describe what is included—and excluded—for each of her costs. She'll also want to predict any expected variations.

Documenting your estimates and assumptions also helps you evaluate any new information you gather later in the process. You can easily compare it against the information you used for your original analysis.

Step 4: Analyze the Alternatives

You've gathered data on your alternatives and estimated time frames for implementing each choice. Now you need to carefully analyze the alternatives you identified using the data you've collected. To do this, you evaluate each alternative against your metrics and create a framework for comparing alternatives.

Evaluating alternatives against your metrics

In most companies, executives want to know the financial implications of each of the alternative courses of action presented to them in a business case. That is, they want to know an alternative's possible impact on revenues, its return on investment for the time period you selected, its payback period (when its benefits will pay for the resources invested in it), and so forth.

Many managers who lack a strong financial background worry about their ability to provide this information in their business case. You won't necessarily do such financial analyses yourself—unless, of course, you want to do them. If you don't, ask someone in the finance department or a peer who is an expert in finance for help.

You ultimately want to show each alternative's impact on the metrics you've defined, as well as on the financial metrics and other metrics of interest to top management. That's why it's helpful to understand a few common financial metrics.

Understanding common financial metrics

The following are some financial metrics that, in most organizations, are of great interest to high-level executives:

- **Payback period:** The time that transpires before an investment pays for itself; the length of time needed to recoup the cost of an investment.

- **Net present value (NPV):** The economic value of an investment. You calculate NPV by subtracting the cost of the investment in your proposed alternative from the present value of the investment's future earnings. Because of the time value of money, the investment's future earnings must be discounted in order to be expressed accurately in today's dollars.

- **Return on investment (ROI):** A financial ratio measuring the cash return from an investment relative to its cost for a stated period of time.

Choose the financial and nonfinancial business performance metrics and calculations that best meet the needs of your audience and are most appropriate for your business case.

Creating a framework for comparing alternatives

At this point in building your case, you've estimated each of your alternative's financial ramifications and considered their impact on any nonfinancial metrics you've defined. Now document your conclusions so they are easy to compare. Try to turn as many conclusions as possible into specific dollar amounts.

Not every alternative has potential impacts that can be expressed as dollars or measurable improvement in business metrics, however. In such cases, consider creating a pros and cons table. Use this table to capture positive financial outcomes and nonfinancial advantages as well as any negative financial outcomes and nonfinancial disadvantages. Although many organizations have prescribed formats for evaluating and comparing alternatives, starting with a simple pros and cons table is an easy way to document your thinking in one place. Even if you have a set of financial and nonfinancial metrics, it is important to also do a pros and cons table.

Let's consider Sydney's framework for comparing her three alternatives. Before creating a pros and cons table, Sydney gathered the following information on her three alternatives and made a series of assumptions. (Depending on the scope of your business case, you may not need to perform such a thorough analysis.)

Sydney's alternative 1: Hire a consulting firm. Sydney's analysis for her first alternative—hire a consulting firm—yielded the following assumptions:

- Impact on sales: Sydney found a consulting firm that specializes in solutions selling. She asked Satellite's vice president of sales for an estimate on how using the consulting firm's methods would affect sales. He estimated that this choice would result in a 10 to 20 percent increase in sales. Her competitors saw increases of about 10 percent. Sydney decided to use the 10 percent number for her analysis, which translated into $7 million in additional sales by the end of year 1.

- **Costs:** The cost to hire the firm for one year would be $2 million.

- **Impact on customer satisfaction:** Sydney believed that the consulting firm would be more effective at improving customer satisfaction because of its experience in this area. A partner at the firm estimated that customer satisfaction would improve by 10 to 15 percent. She selected 10 percent because she could not confirm whether this firm inflated its expected results, and she wants to provide stakeholders with realistic numbers.

- **Impact on employee satisfaction:** Sydney also assumed that sales employees' satisfaction would increase 10 percent owing to the expected higher sales and resulting higher compensation. However, she believed that some members of her team might be upset that a consulting firm was hired to do their work, which might decrease employee satisfaction. As a result, one to two members of the training group might leave if she chose this option.

- **Impact on turnover:** She consulted HR, which estimated a cost of $50,000 to hire and train two new employees in her group if staff did leave.

Sydney's alternative 2: Add two contractors, with the possibility of hiring them permanently later. Sydney's analysis for her second alternative—add two contractors, with the possibility of permanent hires later—yielded the following assumptions:

- **Impact on sales:** If Sydney hired contractors and oversaw the project herself, she estimated she would not be as effective as the consulting firm, because she has not managed this type of transition before. She therefore estimated she would get an increase of $5 million in sales by the end of year 1.

- **Costs:** Hiring two contractors for a year would cost $500,000.

- **Impact on customer satisfaction:** Sydney feared that customers wouldn't be as satisfied with the results produced by contractors as with those generated by consultants who were experts in the area. She therefore estimated that customer satisfaction would improve only 5 percent.

- **Impact on employee satisfaction:** She assumed sales employee satisfaction would increase 10 percent, again owing to the higher sales and therefore higher compensation.

Sydney's alternative 3: Status quo (do the training with her existing staff). Sydney's analysis for her final alternative—the status quo—yielded the following assumptions:

- **Impact on sales:** Because her group didn't have experience implementing this new approach, she estimated that it would take them six months longer than the consulting firm to complete the project. She also believed that her group would not produce the same quality of work as the consulting firm. Thus she estimated a sales increase of only $4 million per year. She also estimated that because of her group's previous commitments and steep learning curve, this increase would not start until eighteen months into the project.

- **Impact on customer satisfaction:** She estimated that customer satisfaction would be similar to that of the contracting option—a 5 percent increase.

- **Impact on employee satisfaction:** Sales employee satisfaction would increase 10 percent, as in the other two options.

- **Impact on turnover:** Because her staff was already over-extended, Sydney estimated that it would take at least three months before she and her group could focus any attention on developing the new training. Once the effort began, she believed that her existing staff might become so overwhelmed that one to two members might leave, thus incurring a cost of $50,000 to hire and train two new employees. During those three months, she estimated that at least one sales professional would leave in search of higher commissions at a competitor that had already implemented the solutions-selling approach.

Sydney's pros and cons table. After making these analyses, Sydney developed a table showing each alternative's strengths and weaknesses. Table 1 shows the results of this effort.

"Steps for analyzing alternatives" offers additional suggestions for comparing your different possible courses of action.

TABLE 1

Sydney's pros and cons

Alternative	Pros	Cons
Hire a consulting firm	• $7 million increase in sales per year by the end of year 3 • Customer satisfaction up 10% • Sales team satisfaction up 10% • Consulting firm expertise • Consultant easily replaced by colleague from firm • Option may have more credibility with senior managers because of the firm's experience doing this kind of work	• $2 million cost for one-year contract • Possible cost of $50,000 to hire and train two training and development employees to replace defectors
Add two contractors (with possibility of permanent hires later)	• $5 million increase in sales per year by the end of year 3 • Customer satisfaction up 5% • Sales team satisfaction up 10%	• $500,000 cost for one year • Time required to hire and bring contractors up to speed • Uncertainty about contractors' expertise • Costly (time and money) to replace if not performing
Status quo (use existing staff)	• $4 million increase in sales per year by end of year 3—with a delay of an additional six months over the other two options • No increase in expenses or headcount	• Implementation of training will take six months longer than the other two options, delaying the increases in revenue, customer satisfaction, and sales employee satisfaction

Alternative	Pros	Cons
	• Customer satisfaction up 5% • Sales team satisfaction up 10%	• Potential cost of $50,000 to hire and train two training and development employees to replace defectors • $120,000 in lost sales revenue and in hiring and training costs to replace a defecting sales associate

Steps for analyzing alternatives

1. **List the costs.** Start by thinking about all of the costs that might be associated with each alternative. Identify the up-front costs as well as those you might expect in subsequent years. Make sure to think beyond the obvious financial costs such as purchasing equipment or paying salaries. Consider the business objectives you chose to evaluate and how each alternative will affect them. For example, will the alternative negatively affect employee turnover? If so, can you quantify it? You'll probably need to do research to come up with the relevant numbers. Ask for help from people in other departments such as finance or sales. Also consider looking at industry reports and on the Internet for estimates. Remember to record your sources of information and list any assumptions you make as you go along.

2. **List the benefits of expected additional revenues.** Again, consider the business objectives you've chosen. What benefits do you anticipate resulting from each alternative? How will these benefits affect revenues? For example, how will your project affect customer satisfaction? Can you make a correlation between improved customer satisfaction and an increase in sales? Additional revenues might come from either obtaining new customers or from increased purchases from existing customers. Make sure to consider any costs associated with obtaining these revenues and add them to your list of costs described above.

3. **Point out any cost savings to be gained.** Consider how implementing each alternative could save the organization money. Spend some time thinking about this area because cost savings can be difficult to recognize. They can arise from a variety of sources. For example, will fewer people be required to do a job because of your project? Will your project reduce the time it takes to complete a task, therefore allowing for more work to be completed or more products to be manufactured?

4. **Identify when you expect to see the costs and anticipated revenues.** Look at your three lists and try to estimate when you expect to realize each item on the list. Remember that costs and revenue increases will probably occur incrementally. For example, you might expect revenues to increase by 20 percent in the first year, achieving a 100 percent increase by the end of year 3. Completing this step will also help when you create your implementation plan.

5. **List the impacts on other corporate metrics, such as customer satisfaction, customer retention, and operational**

efficiency. When looking at the impacts of any opportunity on an organization or business, it is important to identify all of the business metrics that your solution may affect. Some of those metrics are financial. But in most companies today, there are other strategic metrics as well, such as customer satisfaction or retention, employee satisfaction or retention, and operating metrics, including cycle time. Many of these metrics ultimately lead to a financial impact. Therefore, identify all of the key corporate metrics that might be affected by your solution. For example, solutions selling might lead to an increased retention of customers who understand the value of the solutions to them.

6. **List any unquantifiable benefits and costs.** Most business cases aren't built on numbers alone. Depending on the business objectives you chose to use for your analyses, you will probably have some qualitative factors to consider as well—for example, the strategic fit of each alternative with your organization's mission, or an increase in community goodwill because of a particular action. Other factors to consider include the ability to take on the new opportunity without losing focus, and the likelihood of success given market conditions. Even without numbers associated with them, these costs and benefits can be persuasive and are important to consider.

7. **Conduct your business impact analyses.** How does each of your alternatives affect finances? Once you have a list of costs and benefits and have quantified as many factors as possible, it's time to run the numbers. Depending on the metrics you have chosen, you might consider calculating the return on investment payback period or net present value. You might also consider a

break-even analysis. You don't need to do these analyses yourself. Instead, ask a colleague for help (e.g., someone in your finance department). Identify the impact on other key business metrics such as customer satisfaction, employee satisfaction, or operations.

8. **Organize the information into a table for comparison.** Once you have all of the information, put it into a table to help you compare your options. One format to consider is the pros and cons table because it is easy to use when you have both quantifiable and unquantifiable costs and benefits.

Step 5: Make a Choice and Assess the Risk

A fter analyzing all the data on your various alternatives, you need to choose the alternative that seems to be the best, and then assess any risks associated with it. By assessing the risks, you can decide how you might mitigate them and whether you should modify your recommended course of action to reduce the risk.

Selecting the best solution

Once you've compared the pros and cons of your alternatives, you'll need to select the best possible solution—and justify your choice. Some companies track data on how various metrics affect their overall financial performance (for example, how customer satisfaction influences sales). If your company has this information and you can attach dollar figures to each of your metrics, then your selection process may be as simple as adding up all the numbers and making a comparison.

However, you probably won't have all of this information at hand. You'll need to come up with a strategy for making your choice. This isn't an exact science, so you'll have to rely on your intuition and best judgment, as well as input from others. Remember to document your rationale so you can explain it to others later.

In the Satellite example, Sydney reviews her pros and cons table and identifies the choice whose benefits she thinks best outweigh the costs: hiring the consulting firm. She reasons that this option would

- Generate the highest revenue increase in the quickest time.

- Give the company access to expertise that would reduce the risks inherent in introducing a new selling strategy.

- Yield the highest increase in customer satisfaction.

- Improve sales employee satisfaction and thus reduce turnover (and possibly attract talent) in the long term.

What Would YOU Do?

Business Is A-Buzz at BuzziBee Learning

AURA IS A PRODUCT MANAGER at BuzziBee Learning. Her division produces BuzziReader, a series of online reading products used in elementary schools. For the past three quarters, her product line's sales have remained flat, so Laura is looking for ways to grow revenues to stay competitive.

Laura believes there are many alternatives for increasing BuzziReaders' sales. For example, the BuzziReader product line could be sold into new markets. Or, the company could create product-line extensions such as printed workbooks to accompany their online products.

Laura builds a strong opportunity statement: "The BuzziReader product line needs to identify the best approach for increasing BuzziBee Learning's revenues." She then convenes a workgroup to explore alternatives for increasing revenues. The group brainstorms a full range of possibilities and then narrows the options to the following:

- Translating BuzziReader products and selling them in new international markets

- Developing a set of BuzziReader workbooks to be used in conjunction with the online programs

- Trying to get the sales force to sell more aggressively in its current markets (the status quo)

Next, she meets with her boss, Martin, to get his input. She learns that he has been interested in BuzziBee getting more involved in overseas markets. He is less enthusiastic about developing workbooks and is not optimistic that pushing the sales force to sell more aggressively would be successful. Martin encourages Laura to explore the options and to "build her case for key decision makers." She wonders what this means, exactly.

What would YOU do? The mentor will suggest a solution in *What You COULD Do.*

Weighing the risks

Once you select an option, identify the potential risks to you and the organization before you commit to it. Think about the risks to the following:

- **The implementation of your idea.** Do you have the right people to accomplish the necessary tasks? Can you meet the necessary schedule with your resources? What would happen to the organization if you cannot meet your goals and timelines?

- **Your peers and organization.** What would happen to your peers and the organization if you don't make the numbers you expected? For example, if your projections are built into your organization's metrics and are rolled up to the corporate commitments for the head of sales, could his or her career suffer if you don't achieve the projected gains? Are there other risks in terms of members of the sales team leaving the organization once they have higher skill levels?

- **You.** What are the possible career consequences if your alternative fails? For example, depending on the size of the project and the amount of resources you need, your performance rating might be affected, you could lose credibility, or you could be let go.

Also consider your personal tolerance level for risk, as well as your organization's tolerance level. In addition, ask someone in your finance department to help you analyze what would happen if you changed some of your assumptions or your estimates changed.

This process is known as sensitivity analysis. For example, what would happen to your organization's bottom line if sales revenue increased only 5 percent instead of the 15 percent you predicted—or if it increased by 20 percent? You might decide that the alternative you've chosen to advocate would no longer be feasible.

Another way to conduct a sensitivity analysis is to describe a worst-case and best-case scenario, and to share both of them in your business case.

> *What you have to do and the way you have to do it is incredibly*
> *simple. Whether you are willing to do it is another matter.*
> —Peter F. Drucker

Deciding how to mitigate the risks

Consider how you might mitigate the risks you've identified. For example, in the Satellite scenario, Sydney reasons that hiring contractors is time consuming: she may not be able to find anyone with the right expertise to do this type of project right away. Therefore, this alternative poses the risk of delaying revenue gains three to six months beyond the consulting option. If this occurred, the sales group wouldn't meet its target numbers for the year. Sydney considers whether to eliminate this option, even though the cost of hiring the contractors would be far less than hiring the consulting firm.

Sydney also thinks about the risk inherent in negotiating the contract with the consulting firm. The consulting firm might want more than $2 million to do the work. To mitigate this risk, she considers using Satellite's best negotiator or even involving her company's vice president of procurement to ensure a well-handled negotiation.

Determining whether to modify your recommended course of action

Deciding how you mitigate risks helps you refine your recommendation even further. If two of your alternatives offer roughly equal benefits, you may want to compare their risks. If your initial recommendation is too risky, you may decide to modify it or even abandon it for a different alternative.

For example, based on her initial analysis, Sydney was leaning toward the option of hiring two contractors. But after considering the risks, she thinks about hiring the consulting firm instead and then hiring two contractors to maintain training and support for sales.

Also keep in mind that for any alternative that requires an increase in headcount or budget dollars, your request for additional resources could be denied. Prepare another option, even if it seems less desirable. Clearly define the negative impact and missed opportunities that would result if resources were not allocated toward your project.

In Sydney's case, if her request for funding to hire the consultancy is refused, she might have to resort to using her own people to implement the new training. She would then be forced to drop several projects so her staff could take on the new project without becoming overloaded. This decision would be especially problematic because her boss has told her that no current projects could be eliminated or delayed.

"Steps for choosing a final recommendation" offers more guidance on this step.

Steps for choosing a final recommendation

1. **Select a preliminary recommendation.** Review the alternatives you've developed. Compare and contrast their pros and cons. Which of your alternatives best supports your organization's business objectives? Which of these stated objectives are most important to your organization? Think about whether one option would be easier to implement than the others. Also, be sure to weigh unquantifiable factors. For example, if the return on investment is similar for two alternatives, you might want to give more consideration to strategic fit when making your final decision. If you have difficulty narrowing your choice to one option at this stage, you can keep the two best options and work from there.

2. **Document the rationale for your decision.** Once you've made your decision using your best judgment, it is important to explicitly document the rationale for your decision. Do this as soon as possible to avoid overlooking any aspect of your decision-making process. Try to create a concise bulleted list of the four to six primary reasons why you selected your option(s) so you will be able to explain them succinctly to stakeholders and decision makers.

3. **Consider the risks.** Identify the potential risks to both you and the organization of implementing your recommended choice(s).

Consider any risks related to your career, the implementation, and your projected numbers. Also consider running some sensitivity analyses to see how your numbers would change using different estimates or assumptions.

4. **Look for ways to mitigate the risks.** After you identify risks, think about how you can mitigate them. For example, could you start with a pilot project to test your assumptions before launching a full-scale implementation? Also, consider whether you have control over the risks associated with your recommended alternative(s). For example, would either fail if a competitor lowered its prices or if the price of a raw material you use in manufacturing increased?

5. **Revisit your original recommendation.** Think about how desirable the outcome of your recommended option(s) would be. For example, would your department's morale increase significantly as a result? Then think about how likely the stated outcome is to occur (i.e., how many risks did you identify and how likely is it that you can control them?). Keep in mind your personal tolerance for risk and also that of your organization. If you have been considering two options until this point, consider which one makes the most sense in light of these factors. It's possible that you might find that yet another option (possibly a combination of alternatives) is actually the most desirable.

What You COULD Do.

Remember Laura's question about how to start building her case with key decision makers?

Here's what the mentor suggests:

What Martin means is that Laura will need the support of key decision makers and stakeholders, such as the directors of sales and finance, to eventually implement her final proposed course of action. For example, to get the money she needs, she'll have to persuade the directors of sales and finance to support the project. If the directors will be budgeting for the coming year in the next few weeks, Laura will need to get her idea to them quickly.

She shouldn't hold off on these preliminary discussions with key stakeholders just because she doesn't have a formal proposal developed yet. By talking with the directors of sales and finance early, she might learn important information that would help her assess her options. For example, a conversation with the director of sales might reveal any existing contracts the company has with international distributors. A chat with the director of finance might unearth the fact that there's less money available for some options than for others.

Laura should also identify any other stakeholders whose collaboration would be critical for successfully implementing her initiative and try to meet with these individuals early in the process as well. These could include people who would have to carry out key tasks in her initiative, such as writing translations, developing workbooks, or stepping up sales efforts.

Step 6: Craft a Plan for Implementing Your Idea

Once you've selected the best alternative and thought about how to manage its risks, your work isn't done. You still need to craft a plan for implementing your idea. For this step, it's important to

- Understand the purpose of an implementation plan

- List your milestones

- Communicate with decision makers about your progress

- Identify resources you'll need to carry out your proposed course of action

- Clarify who will do what to implement your alternative

- Indicate when the alternative will generate the intended benefits

- Track your results

In the pages that follow, we explore each of these tasks in greater depth.

Understanding the purpose of an implementation plan

Your implementation plan lays out how you intend to track your progress and measure your success if your proposed solution is put into action. Many managers think of an implementation plan as a list of action items, due dates, and the people responsible for them. Decision makers reading your business case will certainly want to know this information. But they'll also want to know the following:

- The primary milestones

- The individuals responsible/accountable for each milestone

- The resources required to reach each milestone

- Dates when the company will see the benefits of your recommended course of action

- Impacts on the company's expense and headcount budgets

- Increases in revenue

- Your plan for demonstrating that the solution's intended results have been realized

Keep in mind that while decision makers will want to understand each of your milestones to ensure that your project is feasible, they do not need the details of how you will accomplish each milestone.

Listing your milestones

Begin developing your implementation plan by listing the major steps needed to carry out your solution. (Resist any urge to write down every little detail of your project plan.) These major steps are your milestones. Include notes about how you plan to address any risks. For example, document that you will start with a pilot training project or use a skilled negotiator in the contract phase.

If there are definable phases to the project, consider listing your milestones by phase. In the Satellite example, this list would take the following form:

- **Phase 1 (1 month):** Hire the consultant using the VP of procurement to negotiate the contract.

- **Phase 2 (6 months):** Develop training, conduct pilot training, evaluate pilot, and collect sales results.

- **Phase 3 (3 months):** Roll out training to all salespeople and sales coaches.

- **Phase 4 (1 month):** Track results; forecast improvement in sales, customer value, and employee turnover to establish business results targets for the next year.

- **Phase 5 (ongoing):** Modify financial targets for sales on an ongoing basis.

Communicating with decision makers

Depending on the nature of your proposal, you may also want to establish explicit check-in points with decision makers to assess progress toward your stated goals. These check-in meetings usually occur after completion of a project phase. During the meetings, decision makers review the status of your project and advise you on any needed midcourse corrections.

When you present your milestones to decision makers, expect that they will want the project done much sooner than your estimated final delivery date. Anticipate negotiations about the time frame. Be prepared with a backup plan for how you could complete phases more quickly, or develop a convincing argument for why accelerating the project implementation would be too risky and would not achieve the intended results.

Identifying resources you'll need

Now ask yourself what resources you'll need at each project phase. For instance, in the Satellite scenario, Sydney might expect to need someone from the procurement group to develop and monitor the contract between Satellite and the consulting firm. She will also need $2 million added to her budget to pay for the consulting contract.

Show any movement of budget dollars and headcount as a step in your project plan. Otherwise, it may be overlooked, or decision makers may assume you will fund the project from your current budget.

Clarifying responsibilities

Many projects do not succeed because managers fail to clarify who will be accountable for each milestone and to get a commitment from these individuals. To illustrate, Sydney knows she'll need someone from the procurement group to negotiate the consulting contract. But if she doesn't confirm with the department up front that they can provide someone, she may be left empty-handed when the contract negotiation phase begins.

In your implementation plan, name the individuals who will do each phase of the work. Also indicate who will be responsible for ensuring that each phase of the project realizes its intended results in terms of costs, revenues, benefits, and deliverables. (More than one person may share this responsibility.)

When reviewing your business plan, decision makers will also want to determine what burdens they'll have to shoulder in order for your proposed solution to succeed. For example, in the Satellite scenario, the sales group would need to increase its forecasted revenue commitments to justify the cost of hiring the consulting firm.

Indicating expected payoff

Decision makers reviewing your business case want to know when they can expect your solution to pay off—that is, to generate the promised benefits. To answer this question, look at your data and clearly identify the range of impacts you expect to see during implementation of your solution.

For instance, Sydney expects sales revenue to increase by $7 million once her solution is implemented. Does she anticipate it will rise immediately? Probably not. More likely, she expects it to be flat at first. She believes that 10 percent of the annualized $7 million (or $175,000) will be realized in the third quarter and 30 percent (or $525,000) in the fourth quarter of year 1, 60 percent in year 2 ($4.2 million), and the full $7 million at the end of year 3.

In estimating payoff dates, remember to plan for a lag between the time when results occur and when they are recorded. Although your plan might generate the expected results during the expected period, those results may not get recorded in your company's performance management system until the following period.

Tracking your results

The projections in your implementation plan will help you sell your case to decision makers. They will also provide benchmarks for evaluating your project's effectiveness once it's implemented.

If your recommended solution receives the go-ahead, your organization will want you to regularly report on the project's successes and shortfalls. By keeping track of your estimated due dates versus the actual delivery dates, as well as estimated benefits versus actual benefits, you will generate the data you'll need to garner support for your project through each of its milestones.

Tracking your project's results will also help you strengthen your ability to build sound business cases and lead projects. To illustrate, once your project rolls into action, it may generate results that far exceed your expectations—signaling that you might have been too conservative in your business case. Or, you could see results that fall far short of your forecasts—suggesting that you may have been overly ambitious.

Whether your results prove better or worse than your expectations, take time to identify the causes behind any major deviation from your business case. By understanding what went wrong, you can learn what to do differently in the future. And by identifying what worked, you derive successful practices to use in subsequent efforts.

See "Tips for creating an implementation plan" for additional helpful guidance on this step in developing a business case.

Tips for creating an implementation plan

- Consider all of the steps it will take to make your project a reality, but include only major milestones in the case you present to decision makers. This audience does not need a high level of detail.

- Make sure your milestones can be clearly defined and easily measured—for example, "develop pilot training content" or "conduct market testing."

- Use generic rather than specific dates—for example, "year 1" or "six months from contract approval."

- Be realistic about the time it will take to implement your recommendation. Managers often underestimate the time they'll need.

- Consider the resources you'll need for each milestone and whether they will be available for your project. For example, is it likely that someone from sales will be available to help review your training program? If not, who else could help you?

- Be prepared for decision makers to ask you to speed up the implementation. Have a backup plan for how you could do things more quickly or a convincing set of reasons why it is too risky to push the dates up.

- Use specific names, not just department names or position titles, when assigning accountability for a task or committed result.

Step 7:
Communicate
Your Case

You've crafted an implementation plan for your proposed course of action. Now it's time to take the final step in developing your business case: communicating it to decision makers. Keys to this step include understanding your audience and presenting your business case effectively, including making smart use of visuals.

Understanding your audience

Building a business case is hard work. You may feel tempted to explain every detail of all that work to your decision makers while presenting your case to them. Resist that urge. In presenting your case, you want to deliver a short, focused sales pitch, not a lengthy, detailed lecture—even if your written business case contains rich detail.

Who will decide whether to approve your proposed solution? You'll need to sell your case to the decision makers—and to those who influence them. The following tactics can help you:

- **Clarify what you want them to do.** What do you want from each individual in your audience? Do you want them to approve resources? Do you want them to talk up your proposal to others? Clearly state your need.

- **Identify what they value and care about most.** Do they care about ROI? Customer satisfaction? Some other measurement of business performance? You identified your stakeholders' business objectives early in the process of building your business case. Now tailor your pitch to highlight the expected results and metrics that are *most* important to each decision maker.

- **Articulate what they stand to gain.** Explain how your audience will benefit if your idea is implemented. For example, perhaps the vice president of sales will get his staff up to speed more quickly or exceed sales targets if your recommendation is put into action.

- **Assess their level of risk tolerance.** Demonstrate that you've considered the risks inherent in your proposed course of action, and explain your plan for mitigating them.

- **Determine how they like to receive information.** What does your audience or your company require for written business cases in terms of format and level of detail? Do the decision makers want cases summarized in three slides—or in a two-page, single-spaced document? Will they require a copy of your case before meeting with you to hear your presentation? Find out, and then give them what they want.

Using visuals to present your case

Check with your finance, strategy, or human resources department to see if your company requires a certain layout for business cases. If it doesn't specify a desired format, you can use the business case template provided in the Tips and Tools section of this book. Even if your company only requires a written document for each business case, consider also creating a visual presentation to help sell your idea.

> *Put the argument into a concrete shape ... round and*
> *solid as a ball, which they can see and handle and carry*
> *home with them, and the cause is half won.*
> —Ralph Waldo Emerson

When created effectively, slide presentations help focus your audience's attention. Because viewing too many slides can be overwhelming to your audience, keep slides to a minimum. Use no more than seven slides to make your case. The slides you'll want to include correspond approximately to the steps you followed to build your business case:

- **Slide 1:** The opportunity statement

- **Slide 2:** The two or three alternatives you considered, as well as the business objectives and performance metrics you chose to measure your alternatives against

- **Slide 3:** A summary of the costs and benefits you considered

- **Slide 4:** Your initial recommendation and why you chose it

- **Slide 5:** The risks associated with this recommendation and how you plan to mitigate them

- **Slide 6:** The high-level milestones you expect to achieve and dates when the organization will realize benefits; persons accountable for each milestone; and resources needed for each milestone

- **Slide 7:** A reiteration of why the opportunity is important and how your recommendation will benefit your organization, including its impact on business results

Don't include formulas and calculations in your slides. Instead, create a few backup slides containing this information, in case someone in your audience asks about them. Listeners tend to lose track of the main idea when the presenter gets too focused on small details. Plan to walk your audience through the presentation and then take time to go more in depth if people have questions.

Be sure to have all your backup information well organized and easily accessible so you are prepared for questions during and after your presentation.

"Tips for writing your business case" provides more ideas for this step.

Tips for writing your business case

- Ask whether your company has a required format for business cases. If it doesn't, consider what format would be best for your particular audience—for example, an executive summary highlighting the key points for upper management.
- Remember that this is a sales pitch. Engage your audience by clearly stating the opportunity up front and selling the opportunity again at the end of your document.

- Clearly illustrate how you've arrived at your recommendation. Documenting each step you've taken will help the reader better understand the reasoning behind your proposal.
- Make it interesting. Remember that someone will have to read your case—your success depends on your ability to tell a convincing story.
- Keep it concise. Your case should be as short as possible while still providing enough detail to give the reader the whole story.
- Use descriptive language (not just a series of bullet points) to help your reader visualize your expected outcomes.
- Demonstrate the value of the project from all points of view— financial, customer, executive, employees, and society as a whole. Tell your reader why this project is important.
- Be clear about what you are asking your audience to do. Do you need resources from them? Do you need their support to get their direct reports to work on your project? Do you need additional headcount, expense dollars, or capital dollars?
- Verify that you have calculated the numbers correctly. Ideally, have the finance department review your calculations and assumptions before you present your case to others.

Tips and Tools

Tools for Developing a Business Case

IDENTIFYING ALTERNATIVES

Use this worksheet to identify alternatives for seizing an opportunity. Before you can identify alternatives, you'll need to first define your opportunity and identify the business objectives and metrics you'll want to use. See "Steps for analyzing alternatives" and "Steps for choosing a final recommendation" for help with comparing your options and making a recommendation.

Part I: Defining the opportunity

Define the opportunity

Briefly describe the problem you want to solve or opportunity you want to seize.

Draft an opportunity statement

Describe the benefits that will come from solving the problem or seizing the opportunity. *For example, answer the question "How will my group/unit/company benefit from spending resources to address this issue?" Be sure to avoid the common mistake of defining the opportunity in terms of a preferred solution.*

Part II: Identifying objectives and metrics

Identify relevant business objectives

List the key business objectives for your organization that are most relevant to the opportunity listed above. To find out what your company considers important, examine the key business metrics it tracks (e.g., customer loyalty, environmental responsibility).

1.	
2.	
3.	
4.	
5.	
6.	

Prioritize your objectives

Narrow your list to three or four objectives by considering your stakeholders. Which objectives are they most likely to consider important, based on their needs and interests? Which objectives do they tend to use as the basis for decision making?

1.	
2.	
3.	
4.	

Identify metrics for each objective

Identify metrics that map to each of your objectives. Once you've determined your alternatives, you'll use these metrics to measure the impact of each of your options. *Sample metrics include customer satisfaction, customer retention, employee satisfaction, turnover, cycle time, costs, and so on.*

1.	
2.	
3.	
4.	

Part III: Generating alternatives

Generate a list of alternatives

What are the alternative courses of action for realizing your opportunity—and meeting key business objectives? Remember that the status quo should always be considered as an option. To ensure that you consider a full set of alternatives, convene a group of stakeholders for a brainstorming session.

1.	
2.	
3.	
4.	
5.	*Status quo option*

Narrow your list of alternatives

List your best two or three options, in addition to the status quo. Use your best judgment to come up with a reasonable set of options that will likely address your business objectives and stakeholders' needs.

1.	
2.	
3.	
4.	*Status quo option*

TRACKING PROJECT IMPLEMENTATION

Use this form to track your project during its implementation. Consider whether you need to make any changes to your implementation plans based on the results you achieve during each phase. You may also use the data you gather in this tool to help you build better-informed business cases in the future.

Phase I

Title of phase:

Description of phase:

Deliverables	Estimated due date	Actual completion date
1.		
2.		
3.		
4.		

Benefits

Estimated level of benefit	Actual level of benefit

Recommended changes for next phase

Phase II

Title of phase:

Description of phase:

Deliverables	Estimated due date	Actual completion date
1.		
2.		
3.		
4.		

Benefits	
Estimated level of benefit	Actual level of benefit

Recommended changes for next phase

Phase III

Title of phase:

Description of phase:

Deliverables	Estimated due date	Actual completion date
1.		
2.		
3.		
4.		

Benefits	
Estimated level of benefit	Actual level of benefit

Recommended changes for next phase

Phase IV

Title of phase:

Description of phase:

Deliverables	Estimated due date	Actual completion date
1.		
2.		

3.		
4.		

Benefits

Estimated level of benefit	Actual level of benefit

Recommended changes for next phase

CHECKLIST FOR CREATING A BUSINESS CASE

Use the twenty questions in the checklist below to evaluate your preparedness for drafting a written business case.

Question	Yes	No
1. Have you defined a clear problem you want to solve or opportunity you want to seize?		
2. Have you developed a clear opportunity statement?		
3. Have you identified key business objectives for your organization that are relevant to this opportunity?		
4. Have you narrowed your list of objectives by considering your stakeholders' needs and interests?		
5. Have you identified metrics that map to each of your business objectives?		
6. Have you generated a full list of alternatives to meet your opportunity by brainstorming with stakeholders?		
7. Have you narrowed your alternatives to those that best address your objectives and key stakeholder needs?		
8. Have you gathered all the data you'll need to be able to analyze your alternatives?		
9. Have you estimated a time frame for implementing the initiative and achieving the benefits of your opportunity?		
10. Have you documented all your estimates and assumptions?		
11. Have you analyzed your alternatives against relevant business metrics?		
12. Have you compared your alternatives using a pros and cons table or other framework?		
13. Have you selected the best possible solution given your analysis?		
14. Have you considered the risks—and developed a mitigation plan for each risk?		
15. Have you created a high-level implementation plan?		

16. Have you created a tracking plan or other means of tracking project results?		
17. Do you know who will ultimately decide whether to approve your recommended solution?		
18. Do you know the best way to sell your case to the decision makers identified in question 17?		
19. Have you considered ways to keep your final presentation focused and concise?		
20. Do you have all the backup data (including calculations) you'll need if someone requests further detail?		

If you answered "yes" to all of these questions, you are probably prepared to make your case. If you answered "no" to any questions, you may want to wait to present your case until you can answer "yes" to those questions.

BUSINESS CASE TEMPLATE

Use this template as a guide for drafting your own business case.

Proposed project/initiative title

Description of proposed project/initiative

Business opportunity

Potential impact of business results

Alternatives chosen for analysis

Assumptions

Analysis of alternatives

Alternative 1:	
Pros	Cons

Alternative 2:		
Pros		**Cons**

Alternative 3:	*Status quo*	
Pros		**Cons**

Recommendation and rationale

Recommendation

Rationale

Risks and mitigation plans

Risks	Plan

Implementation plan		
Phase 1:		
Phase/Milestone description		
Deliverables	**Due date**	**Accountable person**
Resources needed		
Expected level of benefit		
Phase 2:		
Phase/Milestone description		
Deliverables	**Due date**	**Accountable person**
Resources needed		
Expected level of benefit		
Phase 3:		
Phase/Milestone description		
Deliverables	**Due date**	**Accountable person**

Resources needed

Expected level of benefit

Phase 4:

Phase/Milestone description

Deliverables	Due date	Accountable person

Resources needed

Expected level of benefit

Phase 5:

Phase/Milestone description

Deliverables	Due date	Accountable person

Resources needed

Expected level of benefit

Test Yourself

This section offers ten multiple-choice questions to help you identify your baseline knowledge of developing a business case.

Answers to the questions are given at the end of the test.

1. When creating an implementation plan for your business case, it is generally advisable to do all of the following *except*?

   a. Include people's names when assigning accountability for a task.

   b. Use specific due dates for each milestone.

   c. Clearly describe your milestones.

2. In which of the following situations would you prepare a business plan instead of a business case?

   a. To demonstrate the value a new product offering brings to the organization.

   b. To decide how to prioritize projects in your group and which ones to eliminate.

   c. To plan how your business unit will change over the next five years to adapt to competition.

3. You've defined an opportunity and identified several viable alternatives. Which of the following is the *best* strategy for narrowing those options?

    a. Eliminate any choices that are likely to be unpopular with a key stakeholder.

    b. Eliminate elaborate, high-risk options.

    c. Eliminate the status quo option if it seems unlikely.

4. Which of the following statements about the data-gathering and analysis phases of building your business case is accurate?

    a. Much of the information you gather relies on estimates and assumptions.

    b. All of the information you'll need can be gained by talking with stakeholders.

    c. The return on investment (ROI) should be the primary financial driver for your decision making.

5. You've analyzed your alternatives for pursuing a particular business opportunity. What is the *best* next step?

    a. Draft a high-level implementation plan.

    b. List the risks associated with each alternative.

    c. Identify a rationale for making a decision.

6. Your colleague, Jack, has made a business case for a project that requires help from outside consultants. He received approval for the project, but the finance department never transferred money for the consultants' fees to his budget. He most likely failed to:

a. Establish who would be accountable for the project and get a commitment from these individuals.

b. Clearly identify the need to add money to his budget in order to implement the project.

c. Choose a feasible alternative.

7. Which of the following is *not* good advice for presenting your business case to decision makers?

a. Include all your calculations up front to show the depth of your analysis.

b. Be concise so your audience focuses on the most important information.

c. Tell a convincing story using descriptive language.

8. Which of the following is the *best* definition of a business case?

a. A document that presents the rationale for a decision you've made.

b. A guide to how an organization will navigate through a changing business landscape.

c. A tool for identifying and considering multiple alternatives before recommending one option.

9. You've defined the opportunity for your business case. What is the *best* next step?

a. Generate a list of possible alternatives for addressing this opportunity.

b. List the business objectives you think key stakeholders will likely support.

c. Consider how this opportunity could help your company meet vital business goals.

10. You must be able to express each alternative's potential impact in dollar amounts. True or false?

a. True.

b. False.

Answers to test questions

1, b. You should try to use generic due dates rather than specific due dates in a business case—for example, "year 1" or "six months from contract approval." Specific dates are not usually necessary at this stage of developing your business case. Moreover, it is not advisable to lock yourself into meeting particular due dates early in the process. If you commit to certain dates on paper, you may be held accountable for achieving them—even if they are not realistic.

2, c. You would use a business plan to anticipate how your business unit will change over the next five years to adapt to the competitive market. Business plans generally feature long-range projections of revenues, expenses, and other information needed to secure financing from investors or to plan strategy execution. A business *case*, on the other hand, focuses on a single action or decision and its alternatives. Managers create business cases to gain support for all manner of decisions, to initiate action, or to obtain resources for a specific initiative.

3, b. Once you have generated a list of alternatives, use your intuition to come up with a reasonable subset of alternatives that will likely address your most important business objectives and stakeholder needs. One strategy for narrowing your list of alternatives is to eliminate any options that seem excessively complicated or difficult to implement and to retain more feasible choices.

4, a. Much of the information-gathering and analysis process requires you to make estimates and assumptions. Do your best to come up with information that seems sensible and that you can defend. Be sure to document your estimates and assumptions so you can explain your reasoning to anyone who asks.

5, c. Once you analyze your alternatives, the next step is to identify a rationale for making your decision. Selecting a decision-making rationale isn't an exact science, so you'll have to rely on your intuition and best judgment. Remember to document your rationale so you can explain it to others later.

6, b. One common mistake managers make when creating a business case is failing to spell out the need for additional resources in the implementation plan. If decision makers are not explicitly informed of the need for resources, they may approve the project but fail to allocate the necessary resources. If you don't show any movement of budget dollars and headcount as a step in your implementation plan, it may be overlooked—or stakeholders will assume that you will fund the project from your own budget.

7, a. One of the most common mistakes managers make is trying to convey too much information up front when presenting their business case to decision makers. It is tempting to try to demonstrate how much work and thought went into your decision, but resist the urge. Most executives are busy, and they only want to see the information they need to make a decision. You may want to create backup slides or include an appendix in your document that presents calculations and additional analysis for people who desire more detailed information.

8, c. A business case answers the question "What happens if we take this course of action?" For example, if your unit is considering expanding sales to a new market, your boss might ask, "Which of three alternative markets should we invest in to create the most value—and should we even make this investment?" Managers at all levels create business cases to gain support for various types of decisions, to initiate action, or to obtain resources for an initiative.

9, c. After defining the opportunity for your business case, your next step should be determining how that opportunity would enable your company to achieve its most important objectives. To find out what your company considers important, examine the key business metrics it tracks. Once you have identified several business objectives relevant to your company, prioritize them and choose three or four to use for your business case. To narrow the field, consider whose support you'll need and who would be affected if your ideas were put into action. Spend time determining how these key stakeholders tend to make decisions and what business results are most important to them.

10, b. Most business cases aren't built on numbers alone. In fact, many companies place high value on benefits that may be difficult to quantify, such as increased customer goodwill because of an action you're proposing. You might not be able to attach a specific dollar amount to certain costs and benefits, but their impact might still be persuasive. In such cases, consider creating a pros and cons table for your alternatives to capture any positive and negative financial and nonfinancial impacts.

To Learn More

Articles

Lovett, Paul D. "Meetings That Work: Plans Bosses Can Approve." *Harvard Business Review* OnPoint Enhanced Edition. Boston: Harvard Business School Publishing, February 2000.

A plan meeting is where people make the decision to go forward with an idea or not. Yet managers often overload a plan presentation with unimportant facts or simply supply inadequate information. CEOs want four questions answered before they'll approve a plan: What is the plan? Why is it recommended? What are its goals? How much will it cost? You should be able to answer each of these questions clearly and in a way that can lead to an agreed-upon course of action.

Mankins, Michael C., and Richard Steele. "Stop Making Plans; Start Making Decisions." *Harvard Business Review* OnPoint Enhanced Edition. Boston: Harvard Business School Publishing, January 2006.

Many executives have grown skeptical of strategic planning. Strategic planning fails because of two factors: it typically occurs annually, and it focuses on individual business units. A few forward-looking firms have thrown out their calendar-driven, business-unit-focused planning procedures and replaced them with continuous, issues-focused decision making. In doing so, they rely on several basic principles: They separate, but integrate, decision making and plan making. They focus on a few key themes. And they structure strategy reviews to produce real decisions. When companies change the timing and focus of strategic planning, they also change the nature of senior management's discussions about strategy—from "review and approve" to "debate and decide," in which top executives actively think through every major decision and its implications for the company's performance and value.

Obuchowski, Janice. "A Winning Proposition." *Harvard Management Communication Letter,* July 2005.

When putting together a proposal, many business people start off with their company's history, trot out its mission statement, and then discuss the company's philosophy before ever addressing the most crucial thing: the potential customer. The result is a generic document stuffed with boilerplate text—text that will be largely unread. For a proposal to be effective, it must be written with the prospective customer firmly in mind, and it must offer a solution that's tailor-made to that prospective customer's needs.

O'Leary, John. "Learn to Speak the Language of ROI." *Harvard Management Update,* October 2002.

Nobody is getting approval to spend money these days unless he or she can demonstrate an economic return for the company. Thus, nonfinancial professionals are now having to master the mysterious language of return on investment (ROI). This article provides expert advice on what you need to know about the basics of ROI to get your next budget approved.

Rich, Stanley R. and David E. Gumpert. "How to Write a Winning Business Plan." *Harvard Business Review* OnPoint Enhanced Edition. Boston: Harvard Business School Publishing, January 2001.

A well-conceived business plan is essential to the success of an enterprise. Whether you are starting up a venture, seeking additional capital for an existing product line, or proposing a new activity for a corporate division, you will have to write a plan detailing your project's resource requirements, marketing decisions, financial projections, production demands, and personnel needs. The plan must reflect the viewpoint of three constituencies: the customer, the investor, and the producer. Too many business plans focus excessively on the producer.

Books

Hammond, John S., Ralph L. Keeney, and Howard Raiffa. *Smart Choices: A Practical Guide to Making Better Decisions.* Boston: Harvard Business School Press, 1999.

Making smart choices is a fundamental life skill, relevant to anyone: managers, doctors, lawyers, teachers, students, parents, young, old. Your decisions will shape and influence the course of your professional career and the quality of your personal life—the ability to make good decisions is a key factor in determining whether you achieve your goals. To help you increase your chances of finding satisfying solutions,

Smart Choices blends the art and science of decision making into a straightforward, proven approach for making tough choices. *Smart Choices* doesn't tell you what to decide; it tells you how. Authors Hammond, Keeney, and Raiffa, among the world's best-known experts on resolving complex decision problems, blend the art and the science of decision making into accessible steps that lead you to consider your choices both intuitively and analytically. Here, for the first time, is a flexible system that can be applied to business decisions, to personal decisions, to family decisions—to any decision you make.

Schmidt, Marty J. *The Business Case Guide*. 2nd ed. Boston: Solution Matrix, 2002.

What must the business case include to ensure credibility—and accuracy? How do I include benefits besides cost savings and increased sales? This practical, step-by-step handbook provides clear, concrete answers to questions like these and dozens of others. Written with the depth and detail that finance and planning professionals require, *The Business Case Guide* is also rich in practical help and examples for those with little or no background in those areas. *The Business Case Guide* has been recognized as a vital resource for those who build the business case since 1999, when the first edition appeared. This new edition also clarifies important differences between cases for businesses, nonprofit organizations, educational institutions, and government and military organizations.

Other information sources

The following Web sites offer helpful information on creating a business case:

www.businesscase.com

www.solutionmatrix.com

www.prosci.com

eLearning

Harvard Business School Publishing. *Case in Point.* Boston: Harvard Business School Publishing, 2004.

Case in Point is a flexible set of online cases, designed to help prepare middle- and senior-level managers for a variety of leadership challenges. These short, reality-based scenarios provide sophisticated content to create a focused view into the realities of the life of a leader. Your managers will experience the following: Aligning Strategy, Removing Implementation Barriers, Overseeing Change, Anticipating Risk, Ethical Decisions, Building a Business Case, Cultivating Customer Loyalty, Emotional Intelligence, Developing a Global Perspective, Fostering Innovation, Defining Problems, Selecting Solutions, Managing Difficult Interactions, The Coach's Role, Delegating for Growth, Managing Creativity, Influencing Others, Managing Performance, Providing Feedback, and Retaining Talent.

Sources for Developing a Business Case

The following sources aided in development of this book:

Hammond, John S., Ralph L. Keeney, and Howard Raiffa. *Smart Choices: A Practical Guide to Making Better Decisions.* Boston: Harvard Business School Press, 1999.

Maluso, Nancy. "The Business Case—Friend or Foe?" *BPR Online Learning Center* (www.prosci.com).

Maluso, Nancy. "The Business Case—The Essential Elements." *BPR Online Learning Center* (www.prosci.com).

Maul, June. Interview on creating a business case. Boston, June 2005.

McFarland, Jennifer. "Behind Every Successful Manager Is a Great Inside Sales Job." *Harvard Management Update,* December 2001.

O'Leary, John. "Learn to Speak the Language of ROI." *Harvard Management Update,* October 2002.

Schmidt, Marty J. *Business Case Essentials: A Guide to Structure and Content.* Boston: Solution Matrix, 2005.

Schmidt, Marty J. *What's a Business Case? And Other Frequently Asked Questions.* Boston: Solution Matrix, 2003.

Shaw, Gordon, Robert Brown, and Philip Bromily. "Strategic Stories: How 3M Is Rewriting Business Planning." *Harvard Business Review,* May–June 1998.

Solution Matrix. "Business Case vs. Business Plan: Do You Know the Difference?" *Cost Benefit Newsletter,* July 25, 2004.

Notes

Notes

Notes

Notes

Notes

Notes

Notes

Notes

Notes

Notes

Notes

Notes

Notes

How to Order

Harvard Business School Press publications are available world-wide from your local bookseller or online retailer.

You can also call:
1-800-668-6780

Our product consultants are available to help you 8:00 a.m.–6:00 p.m., Monday–Friday, Eastern Time. Outside the U.S. and Canada, call: 617-783-7450.

Please call about special discounts for quantities greater than ten.

You can order online at:
www.HBSPress.org